Animal Kingdom Questions and Answers

Fish
A Question and Answer Book

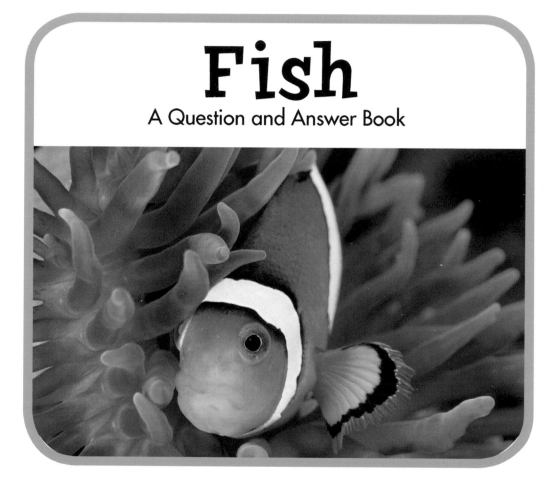

by Isabel Martin

Consulting Editor: Gail Saunders-Smith, PhD

CAPSTONE PRESS
a capstone imprint

Pebble Plus is published by Capstone Press,
1710 Roe Crest Drive, North Mankato, Minnesota 56003
www.capstonepub.com

Library of Congress Cataloging-in-Publication Data
Martin, Isabel, 1977– author.
  Fish : a question and answer book / by Isabel Martin.
      pages cm. — (Pebble plus. Animal kingdom questions and answers)
  Summary: "Simple text and colorful images illustrate types of fish, including common characteristics, diet, and life cycle"—Provided by publisher.
  Audience: Ages 4–8.
  Audience: Grades K–3.
  Includes bibliographical references and index.
  ISBN 978-1-4914-0563-5 (library binding) — ISBN 978-1-4914-0631-1(paperback) — ISBN 978-1-4914-0597-0 (eBook PDF)
  1. Fishes—Miscellanea—Juvenile literature. 2. Children's questions and answers. I. Title.
  QL617.2.M345 2015
  597.02—dc23   2013050346

Editorial Credits
Nikki Bruno Clapper, editor; Cynthia Akiyoshi, designer; Kelly Garvin, media researcher;
Katy LaVigne, production specialist

Photo Credits
Alamy/Joe Austin Photography, 21; Dreamstime/Bluehand, cover, back cover; Minden Pictures: Fred Bavendam, 19, Shinji Kusano/Nature Production, 13; Nature Picture Library/Doug Perrine, 17; Shutterstock: Alexsey Stemmer, 1, Andaman, 15, Durden Images, 7, Krzysztof Odziomek, 11, Mark Caunt, 5, Rich Carey, 9

Note to Parents and Teachers

The Animal Kingdom Questions and Answers set supports national curriculum standards for science related to the diversity of living things. This book describes and illustrates the characteristics of fish. The images support early readers in understanding the text. The repetition of words and phrases helps early readers learn new words. This book also introduces early readers to subject-specific vocabulary words, which are defined in the Glossary section. Early readers may need assistance to read some words and to use the Table of Contents, Glossary, Read More, Internet Sites, Critical Thinking Using the Common Core, and Index sections of the book.

Printed in the United States   5553

Table of Contents

Meet the Fish

Splash! A salmon leaps in a river. Salmon, sharks, eels, and tuna are all fish. These animals come in many shapes, sizes, and colors.

Atlantic salmon

Do Fish Have Backbones?

Yes, fish have backbones.

Rays and sharks have skeletons

made of cartilage. Cartilage bends

more than bone does.

southern stingray

Are Fish Warm-Blooded or Cold-Blooded?

Fish are cold-blooded.

Their body temperature is the same

as the water around them.

spiny sea horse

What Type of Body Covering Do Fish Have?

Most fish have skin covered

with scales. Some scales are smooth.

Other scales are rough. Fish have gills,

fins, and a tail.

How Do Fish Eat?

Most fish eat smaller fish, insects,

crabs, and other animals.

They catch food with their mouths.

Some fish eat plants.

false kelpfish

Where Do Fish Live?

Fish live in lakes, oceans, rivers, and other bodies of water.

Some fish live in freshwater.

Some fish live in salt water.

porkfish (with black stripes)
and grunts

How Do Fish Have Young?

Most fish hatch from eggs.
But some sharks give birth
to live young. The shark babies
grow inside a mother's body
until they are born.

lemon shark baby
and mother

Do Fish Care for Their Young?

Most fish do not care for their young. The baby fish must survive on their own. But some fish do take care of their eggs.

Tasmanian clingfish

eggs

What Is a Cool Fact About Fish?

A walking catfish can move on land.

It digs its fins into the ground

and wiggles like a snake.

This fish can live for a few days

out of water.

walking catfish

Glossary

cartilage—the strong, bendable material that forms some body parts on humans and other animals

cold-blooded—having a body temperature that changes with the surrounding temperature

eel—a fish that looks like a snake

fin—a body part that fish use to swim and steer in water

gill—a body part on the side of a fish; fish use their gills to breathe

hatch—to break out of an egg

ray—a flat fish with eyes on top and a skeleton made of cartilage

scale—one of many small, hard pieces of skin that cover an animal's body

skeleton—the bones (or cartilage) that support and protect the body of a human or other animal

temperature—the measure of how hot or cold something is

Read More

Spilsbury, Louise. *Shark*. A Day in the Life: Sea Animals. Chicago: Heinemann Library, 2011.

Stewart, Melissa. *A Place for Fish*. Atlanta: Peachtree, 2011.

Thomas, Isabel. *Fantastic Fish*. Extreme Animals. Chicago: Raintree, 2013.

Internet Sites

FactHound offers a safe, fun way to find Internet sites related to this book. All of the sites on FactHound have been researched by our staff.

Here's all you do:
Visit www.facthound.com
Type in this code: 9781491405635

Super-cool stuff! Check out projects, games and lots more at
www.capstonekids.com

Critical Thinking Using the Common Core

1. Describe the body parts that help a fish live in water. (Integration of Knowledge and Ideas)

2. Look at the photo on page 7. What kind of skeleton does this fish have? How can you tell? (Key Ideas and Details)

Index

Word Count: 200
Grade: 1
Early-Intervention Level: 16

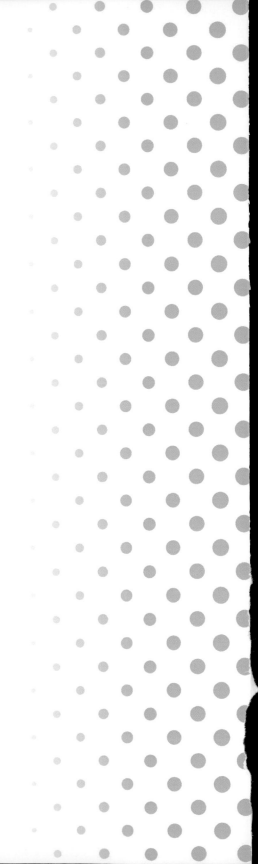